21 Days of Faith Challenge

Living A Life of Faith

Shelley Hitz

21 Days of Faith Challenge

© 2013 by Shelley Hitz

Published by Body and Soul Publishing
Printed in the United States of America
ISBN-13: 978-1-946118-10-3

CONTENTS

Table of Contents

Introduction: 21 Days of Faith Challenge

Appendix

Introduction:
21 Days of Faith Challenge

This year, I want to live a life of faith. I want my faith to be more than simply saying "I believe in God." I want it to be real…a genuine faith that overflows from a heart that is fully trusting in God in every area of my life.

Do You Have Faith?

To be honest, my knee-jerk reaction to this question would be a confident, "Yes!" Why? Well, I have been a Christian for over 20 years. And as a Christian, faith is the foundation of everything I believe.

I grew up as a "PK" (Pastor's Kid) and first surrendered my life to Christ at seven years old. However, I drifted during high school during a rebellious season in my life. I partied, drank to get drunk, and started down a path of destruction. Alcoholism runs on both sides of my family. And so I firmly believe that if God had not intervened, I could have also ended up on that same path. However, through circumstances that I see now as God's intervention in my life, we moved during the middle of my junior year in high school. For the first time, I met other teens that were truly living for Christ in my new school in Findlay Ohio. And their faith in God was not something they were doing for their parents or to look good. It was real. God used these new Christian friends and an organization called Youth for Christ (YFC) to impact my life for eternity. At a YFC event near the end of my junior year in 1992, I decided to live my life for Christ. I cannot explain the change in my life any other way except that God intervened. I was rescued. In fact, as I recall these events, I have tears of gratitude in my eyes for God's mercy on my life. I firmly believe my life would have turned out so much differently had we not moved during my junior year. What I thought would ruin my life, actually saved it.

And so, I have been on this journey of faith in God for over 20 years. Of course I believe in God and have faith. Right?

However, I have to admit that I have struggled with faith lately.

My Struggles with Doubt and Worry

I cannot pinpoint when it happened. But, gradually over the last 18 months, my thoughts began to change from faith in God to doubt. As circumstances in my life turned out much differently than I thought, I became disillusioned and started to wonder if God really had my best interests in mind.

Instead of trusting God with the circumstances of my life, I tried to take things into my own hands. As you can imagine, this led to worry. Worry, worry, and more worry. And as a result, I spent more time doubting God and worrying than I did in believing God and trusting Him with my life.

Ouch.

And with the worry and doubt, came a darkness over my life. Over the last year, I have felt depressed more often than I want to admit. And each time it would come, it felt like I would sink deeper into it.

This is when God led me to do the "21 Days of Gratitude Challenge." And it helped. But, I still felt the darkness settle over me. As I prayed, I realized that it was time to take the next step. It was time for a new challenge. It was time for me to allow God to replace the worry and doubt with trust and faith.

A Year of Faith

And so I sense that this year is to be a year of faith. As I start this 21 Days of Faith Challenge, I know that I need God to empower me to change. I have formed bad habits of worry that I know I cannot change on my own. It will take an empowerment of the Holy Spirit and yet I am willing and ready to cooperate with Him. I am tired of worrying. I am tired of riding a rollercoaster of emotions that jerks me up and down, up and down. I am ready for this next step of faith.

Will You Join Me?

What about you? Will you consider joining me in these 21 Days of Faith? Are you ready to surrender your worries and doubts to God? I have to warn you that this journey will not be easy. But, it will be worth it.

God often speaks to me in illustrations. The picture I see of myself right now is similar to someone who has gotten out of shape physically and is now 40 pounds overweight. After forming bad habits of not exercising and eating junk food, you have to reach a breaking point and be ready to change. Exercising and eating right will not be easy, but it will be worth it.

And in a similar way, I have allowed myself to get out of shape spiritually. I have gained 40 pounds of worry and doubt and have formed bad habits. I am now at a breaking point and am ready to change. Trusting God and believing Him will not be easy, but it will be worth it.

Ready to get started? Let's start with a prayer...

Lord, today I want to thank You for your grace and forgiveness. I confess that I struggle with worry and doubt. Please forgive me for not believing and trusting You. I am ready to change. Empower me with Your Holy Spirit to renew my mind with Your truth and change my thoughts from worry and doubt to thoughts of faith and trust. I thank You for Your unconditional love. Even though I have strayed from the path You have for me, You love me and accept me. Jesus, walk with me as I take this 21 days of faith challenge. I pray that I will not be the same person when it is over but instead a person living a life of faith. I love You. Amen.

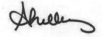

DAY 1

Today is the first day of the faith challenge. Honestly, I feel like I am standing on the edge of a diving board getting ready to jump off. I am both excited and nervous as I commit to taking this challenge. However, one of the first questions we need to ask ourselves is simply, "What is faith?"

Personally, when I think of the word faith, many definitions come to mind. Here are just a few:

- A belief in God
- Stepping out into the unknown
- My thoughts and beliefs
- And so on

I think it would be interesting to ask 100 people this same question, "What is faith?" I am pretty sure there would be MANY different answers depending on each person's background, experiences, and Biblical knowledge. So as we get started, let's look at what the Bible says about faith. To do so, we will look at a well-known scripture from Hebrews 11:1.

"Now faith is the substance of things hoped for, the evidence of things not seen." (NKJV)

From this verse, we see that faith is defined in two ways:

1. The substance of things hoped for and
2. The evidence of things not seen

I also like the way the Amplified version says it.
"Now faith is the assurance (the confirmation, the title deed) of the things [we] hope for, being the proof of things [we] do not see and the conviction of their reality [faith perceiving as real fact what is not revealed to the senses]."
- Hebrews 11:1 (AMP)

Did you catch that? If not, I encourage you to read it again. It says faith is the confirmation or the title deed of the things we hope for.

I am a visual person that learns best through illustrations and so I like how the Amplifed version says that faith is the title deed. Dictionary.com defines title deed as a "deed or document constituting evidence of ownership." Therefore, our faith is like a document that gives evidence of ownership of the things we hope for and those things we do not see. Let's take the illustration a bit further. Faith is like purchasing a home that I have never seen. Even though I have never seen the property or the house, the title deed proves that I am the owner and I can rest confidently in that knowledge.

Martin Luther King Jr. says it this way, "Faith is taking the first step even when you can't see the whole staircase."

Are you ready to live life this way? Trusting God even when you can't see how it will all work out. If so, you will truly be living out a life of faith.

Application:

- Write out Hebrews 11:1 and post it somewhere that you will see it every day throughout this challenge. Read it out loud and meditate on it.
- I encourage you to start a journal that you can write in each day. In your journal, write out what faith means to you. Compare it to the definition we studied in Hebrews 11:1. Are they similar, different? Ask God to reveal to you His definition of faith through His Word.
- For encouragement and accountability in your journey of faith, join our private Facebook group here: www.facebook.com/groups/21daysoffaith

DAY 2

Today God reminded me of a small binder that I started years ago with scriptures and quotes on different topics. My prayer partner at the time mentioned the idea and showed me hers. She said that she keeps her notebook handy and when she is struggling in one of the areas she listed, she will read through the scriptures over and over allowing God to renew her mind with His truth in that particular area.

I loved the idea and decided to start my own.

Believe me, mine is nothing fancy! It is simply a small binder that can hold 3.5 x 5 inch notecards. I even made homemade dividers by simply folding over a piece of scotch tape and writing the topic on it in pen.

I was so glad that I found this little binder today because it contains a quote that I wanted to share with you. Here it is…

"Faith came singing into my room, and other guests took flight. Grief, anxiety, fear and gloom, sped out into the night. I wondered that such peace could be, but faith said gently, *'Don't you see that they can never live with me?'"* ~Elizabeth Cheney

Basically what she is saying in this quote is that faith and worry cannot co-exist. We will either have one or the other.

However, in many Christian circles worry is one of the greatest strongholds in our lives. Why? Well, I think one reason is that we rationalize worry (at least I know that I do) by saying we are "concerned" or have a "heavy burden" for someone. But, if we are really honest to ourselves, many times that "concern" turns to worry so easily.

And worry is a sin.

There. I said it.

Worry is a sin because we are taking our eyes off of Christ and His ability to handle a situation. And when we do this, we are no longer able to live a life of faith.

So, which will it be?
- Faith or doubt?
- Trust or worry?

2 Corinthians 5:7 says, "For we walk by faith, not by sight." (NKJV)

Application:

- Take a moment to say a prayer to God or write it out in your journal. Confess any sin (i.e. doubt, worry, fear, etc.) to God and be as specific as you can. Then, ask God to forgive you and help you to truly repent and turn from your sin. Ask for an empowerment of the Holy Spirit to fill you each day with faith and trust in God.

  Then, anytime you slip back into worry and doubt again, simply bring it to God. Confess your sin again to Him and ask His forgiveness and empowerment to change. Deep habits take time to change, so realize that this may be a minute by minute process at first.

  I encourage you to say this prayer from your heart. But if you want, you can use the following prayer I have written out below.

  Lord, I come to You now admitting that I have allowed other things to take root in my mind and heart. I confess my worry, doubt and fear to You especially in regards to _____ (insert the things that you struggle with the most here). I realize that worry is a sin and that I cannot move forward in my desire for faith until I confess it to you as I am doing now.

I ask You to forgive me and help me to repent and turn from my sin. I want my focus to be on You, not on my circumstances. Empower me through the Holy Spirit to change. Fill me with Your faith and a greater trust in You. I know that this journey will take time but I thank You for your grace and patience with me as I seek more of You in this *21 Days of Faith Challenge*. I love You Lord. In Jesus powerful name I pray, Amen.

DAY 3

There are a lot of things in life that can cause worry and keep us from truly living a life of faith. And it may look different for each one of us. I know one area that triggers worry for me is uncertainty: not knowing what is going to happen or what the future holds. Another big area of worry for me this past year has been finances. For you it may be a relationship in your life or your job. The bottom line? There are a lot of things in life that can trigger worry within us.

I was reading something one day that gave a powerful illustration of what worry can be like. It caught my attention and I now want to share it with you. Here's the illustration: worry is like holding a hand grenade where the pin has already been pulled. Within time, it is going to go off. Therefore, you have two choices.

1. You can hold on to it and allow it to damage you.

Or

2. You can throw it away.

If you throw it away into the direction of other people, it can hurt them and damage them. However, you can also choose to throw it as far away from you and anyone else as possible so that no one gets hurt.

Now, if you were really holding on to a hand grenade where the pin was pulled and you knew it was going to go off in mere seconds, you would get rid of it. You would throw it away. You would get it as far away from you and anyone else as you could to avoid hurting yourself or anyone else.

However, instead, so many times in life we hold on to our worry. We allow it to fester, go off, and cause damage to ourselves or to other people. What a powerful picture that is for us as we embark on this *21 Days of Faith Challenge.*

So, if we truly want to live a life of faith, what should we do when the worry comes?

I Peter 5:7 gives us the answer. "Cast all your anxiety on Him because He cares for you." (NIV)

Jesus wants to take on our worry and anxiety. He is there. He can handle it. He can detonate our "bomb" of worry. He knows what to do with it and He is the One who can handle it. It is time to cast our worries on Him.

"The beginning of anxiety is the end of faith, and the beginning of true faith is the end of anxiety." ~ George Muller

Application:

- Do you have any worry or anxiety that you need to let go of? Are you going to hold onto it until it hurts you or those around you, or will you cast it upon Christ? I encourage you to let go of your worry and cast it upon Him because He cares for you.
- Go through the next 24 hours and take notice of your thoughts. When you identify worry, visualize yourself casting that worry (that circumstance or person, etc.) upon Christ.

  What I do is to actually imagine my worry as a heavy backpack that I take off my shoulders and place in Jesus' hands. I then allow my shoulders to relax as I am no longer the one carrying that worry around but I am trusting it to Jesus and asking Him to handle it.

- Instead of worrying, pray. Then, affirm your trust in God to lead, guide and direct your steps. Sometimes all you need to say is "I trust you Jesus." It sounds simple, but it really is one of the first steps to living a life of faith.

DAY 4

This past 18 months of our lives has been marked with one word…transition. I officially resigned my job as a Physical Therapist at the end of July 2011. Then we moved into a small Toyota RV and lived in 125 square feet of space for 3.5 months…full time. We downsized our earthly belongings and everything we needed fit in either our small RV or our small car.

It was our dream to travel and speak across the country in a RV. However, things didn't work out as we thought or planned. We ended up selling the RV and moving to Colorado instead.

And I was confused.

I had resigned my job as a P.T. to travel and minister and speak full-time with CJ and then…nothing. Silence. It felt like God was silent.

Have you ever experienced a time when God seemed distant or silent in your life?

I think we all experience moments when God seems distant or silent in our lives.

During this current season of transition in my life, it has often felt like I can't see clearly what the next steps will be. I have a strong relationship with Jesus and have had seasons where I could sense His voice and leading clearly in my life.

The picture I get of this season of life is of a fog that has descended over me. I cannot see anything except what is right in front of me...the present moment. I don't know where we will be going and what we will be doing. I don't know how we will pay the bills (although God has provided and we have been able to pay every one of them thus far).

And I Won't Lie to You...It Has Been Hard. Really Hard.

I like to be in control and have a plan. It is difficult to walk by faith. I never realized how much I depended on my regular paycheck from the hospital until we did not have it. I realize now that I was depending more on that steady paycheck than I was on God.

I am not saying that everyone needs to quit their jobs and venture out in faith to learn these lessons. This is simply the path that we have been on these last few months.

And as hard as it has been, it has also been good.

There was a root of self-sufficiency in me that is slowly being uprooted. I am still in the process, but God is teaching me to fully rely on Him and not on my own efforts. He is proving Himself to me over and over as He provides for us something that I never could.

An Illustration of Faith

I woke up to a rainy day just weeks after moving to Colorado and saw something amazing when I looked out our front window. Normally we can see Pikes Peak VERY clearly from our front window. But, that day...nothing. Literally. I could not see the mountain AT ALL. It was almost as if it was not there anymore.

Instantly, God spoke to my heart.

Just because I couldn't see Pikes Peak that morning, didn't mean it was no longer there. The mountain was still there. I know it was because I have seen it so many times in that very same place. It was just that the clouds of that particular day kept the mountain hidden from me.

And So it is With God Sometimes as Well.

There are those bright sunny days where everything seems to be going my way and I can sense God's presence and His voice leading and guiding me so clearly. Then there are other days that seem cloudy and gray, where God seems distant and silent in my life.

It doesn't mean that God isn't there. God is still there. He has proven Himself to me over and over again. It's just that the "clouds" of the day have descended over me at the moment.

And so in those moments when God seems distant or silent, it comes down to trust. Trusting that He's still there, just like I trust Pikes Peak to still be there even though I can't see it clearly from my window.

What does it mean to trust? Well, here's a definition from the dictionary:

Trust (noun)

- reliance on the integrity, strength, ability, surety, etc., of a person or thing; confidence.
- confident expectation of something; hope.

- confidence in the certainty of future payment for property or goods received; credit: to sell merchandise on trust.
- a person on whom or thing on which one relies: God is my trust.
- the condition of one to whom something has been entrusted.

And so, when I am in the midst of the fog, I trust that God is with me.

"Never doubt in the dark what God told you in the light."
~ Raymond Edman

"Never be afraid to trust an unknown future to a known God."
~ Corrie ten Boom

"Trust in the Lord with all your heart and lean not on your own understanding; in all your ways submit to him, and he will make your paths straight."
- Proverbs 3:5-6 (NIV)

Application:

- Can you relate to feeling distant to God? Journal about a time when God seemed distant in your life or share it with a friend.

- Then, choose to trust God today. Even if you are in the middle of a fog and cannot see Him or hear Him clearly, know that He is still there. Affirm your trust in Him by saying a simple prayer, "I trust You, Jesus, even when I cannot see or understand."

DAY 5

Years ago, I received a personalized quote in a picture frame. Even as we were downsizing from our house to a small RV, I decided to keep it. And I am glad I did. God is using it during this season of my life to speak to me.

It says, *"Shelley, Trust Me. I have everything under control. ~ Jesus"*

Many times we need tangible reminders like this to remind us that we can trust Jesus with the circumstances of our lives. Even when we cannot see all the details, He has everything under control.

"When a train goes through a tunnel and it gets dark, you don't throw away the ticket and jump off. You sit still and trust the engineer."
~Corrie ten Boom

"May the God of hope fill you with all joy and peace as you trust in him, so that you may overflow with hope by the power of the Holy Spirit."
- Romans 15:13 (NIV)

Application:

*   Write out this following quote and personalize it with your name. Then, post it somewhere you will see it every day.

    _____ (insert your name),

    Trust Me. I have everything under control.

    ~ Jesus

DAY 6

What does it look like to trust God?

Many times it is easy to talk about faith and trust, but it is hard to visualize how it plays out in our everyday lives. Right before I was to resign my job and launch into full time ministry with CJ, God graciously gave me a picture of what faith looks like. A speaker at a conference demonstrated this illustration so clearly to me.

The speaker stood on the stage and described a season in his family's life when God asked them to step out in faith. He then asked for a volunteer to come up on the stage, directed them to stand up on a table, and then blindfolded them. He turned them around so the volunteer's back was facing the audience.

As he continued to tell his story of trusting God, he quietly began to pull people out of the audience and line them up behind the volunteer. He shared how difficult it was to trust God because he could not see how it would all work out. But, unbeknownst to the speaker, God had a plan developing behind the scenes.

After he lined up around 5-6 people on each side in two parallel lines facing each other, he had them join arms with the person across from them to form a "safety net" behind the volunteer standing on the table. Now remember, all of this was happening quietly and without the knowledge of the volunteer who had been blindfolded.

Finally, the speaker asked the volunteer if he trusted him. The speaker said he had everything under control and was trustworthy. He then asked the volunteer to fall back into a trust fall. However, the volunteer had no idea that there were 10-12 strong and capable people behind him ready to catch him when he fell.

And instantly God spoke to my heart.

Just because I could not see how this next phase of our lives was going to work out, I could trust Him. He was behind the scenes working everything out and providing that "safety net" for CJ and I.

And you know what?

When I reflect back upon the past 18 months of our lives, I can see how we have lived out this illustration. In many ways, it felt like God asked us to stand on a cliff blindfolded and jump off. Finances have been very tight, but we always had what we needed. As my husband has so often reminded me over these last months, there has not been one bill we couldn't pay. We have had food and shelter. God has provided... and sometimes in the most unexpected ways, through means I could never have dreamed, planned or figured out.

I will admit that I have tears in my eyes as I type this out today. Why? Well, even though God has seemed silent during this season of my life, looking back I realize that He was providing for us all along. He has been active in our lives - caring for us in ways I did not, or could not, see at the time.

When we live a life of faith, we may feel like we are walking through our circumstances blindfolded. However, our God sees everything and is able to provide in ways that we cannot even imagine. That is, if we will trust Him.

"God will never, never, never let us down if we have faith and put our trust in Him. He will always look after us. So we must cleave to Jesus. Our whole life must simply be woven into Jesus."
~ Mother Teresa

"Often I have heard people say, 'How good God is! We prayed that it would not rain for our church picnic, and look at the lovely weather!' Yes, God is good when He sends good weather. But God was also good when He allowed my sister, Betsie, to starve to death before my eyes in a German concentration camp. I remember one occasion when I was very discouraged there. Everything around us was dark, and there was darkness in my heart. I remember telling Betsie that I thought God had forgotten us. 'No, Corrie,' said Betsie, 'He has not forgotten us. Remember His Word: For as the heavens are high above the earth, so great is His steadfast love toward those who fear Him.' Corrie concludes, 'There is an ocean of God's love available - there is plenty for everyone. May God grant you never to doubt that victorious love - whatever the circumstances.'"

~ Corrie ten Boom

"Though He slay me, yet will I trust Him."
- Job 13:15 (NKJV)

Application:

- It is easy to trust God in the good times, but more difficult to trust Him during the hard times. In prayer, ask God to help you trust Him regardless of your circumstances.

DAY 7

Many times, Hebrews 11 is called the "Hall of Faith" chapter. I often think of it like the "Hall of Fame" where certain members get inducted. However, the members in God's "Hall of Faith" were chosen due to the faith they demonstrated in their lives.

Here are the names listed within this chapter:

- Abel
- Enoch
- Noah
- Abraham
- Sarah
- Isaac
- Jacob
- Joseph
- Moses
- Rahab
- Gideon
- Barak
- Samson
- Jephthah
- David

- Samuel
- And the prophets

Do you recognize any of these names? I am sure you did! However, today I encourage you to read this entire chapter to learn even more about what faith looks like. And as you do, make sure you don't miss this verse:

"But without faith it is impossible to please Him, for he who comes to God must believe that He is, and that He is a rewarder of those who diligently seek Him."
- Hebrews 11:6 (NKJV)

Do you want to please God? If so, you must have faith! Let's keep seeking to live a life of faith that pleases Him.

"Dependence upon God makes heroes of ordinary people like you and me!"
~Bruce Wilkinson

Application:

- Read Hebrews 11, the "Hall of Faith." Write at least 2 things in your journal that you learn about faith from this chapter.

DAY 8

Today I want to share a story from Mark 9:17-27 (NKJV).

"Then one of the crowd answered and said, 'Teacher, I brought You my son, who has a mute spirit. And wherever it seizes him, it throws him down; he foams at the mouth, gnashes his teeth, and becomes rigid. So I spoke to Your disciples, that they should cast it out, but they could not.'

He answered him and said, 'O faithless generation, how long shall I be with you? How long shall I bear with you? Bring him to Me.' Then they brought him to Him. And when he saw Him, immediately the spirit convulsed him, and he fell on the ground and wallowed, foaming at the mouth.

So He asked his father, 'How long has this been happening to him?'

And he said, 'From childhood. And often he has thrown him both into the fire and into the water to destroy him. But if You can do anything, have compassion on us and help us.'

Jesus said to him, 'If you can believe, all things are possible to him who believes.'

Immediately the father of the child cried out and said with tears, 'Lord, I believe; help my unbelief!'

When Jesus saw that the people came running together, He rebuked the unclean spirit, saying to it: 'Deaf and dumb spirit, I command you, come out of him and enter him no more!' Then the spirit cried out, convulsed him greatly, and came out of him. And he became as one dead, so that many said, 'He is dead.' But Jesus took him by the hand and lifted him up, and he arose."

There is so much we could discuss regarding faith in this passage. However, today I want to focus on the father's response to Jesus. The child's father said, "Lord, I believe; help my unbelief!"

The KJV says it this way, "And straightway the father of the child cried out, and said with tears, Lord, I believe; help thou mine unbelief."

The father cried out with tears.

From this description, the father was definitely NOT feeling complacent or lackadaisical as he responded to Jesus. Instead, he responded with passion and honesty. He was honest that he still struggled with unbelief. But with a passionate plea, he reached out and asked for Jesus' help. And Jesus responded to him by healing his son.

This is a prayer you can also use when you struggle with faith or believing God. Simply say, "Lord, I believe; help my unbelief!"

"Relying on God has to begin all over again every day as if nothing had yet been done."
~C.S. Lewis

Application:

• When faced with doubt and uncertainty, reach out for Jesus' help by praying the simple prayer of the child's father, "Lord, I believe; help my unbelief!"

DAY 9

Have you ever felt like you needed to do something a certain way in order to have faith? I know I have! Well, today I was reminded of the scripture in Hebrews 12:1-2 which talks about where our faith originates. Listen to this...

"Therefore we also, since we are surrounded by so great a cloud of witnesses, let us lay aside every weight, and the sin which so easily ensnares us, and let us run with endurance the race that is set before us, looking unto Jesus, the author and finisher of our faith, who for the joy that was set before Him endured the cross, despising the shame, and has sat down at the right hand of the throne of God." (NKJV)

Now, remember that Hebrews 11 is the "Hall of Faith" chapter which defines faith and describes many heroes of the faith from the Old Testament. So these verses come immediately after that chapter of faith.

And what does it say?

I love how these verses clearly tell us that Jesus is the "author and finisher of our faith." It is not up to us to muster up enough faith for the day. Our faith comes from Christ and not our own efforts.

If you are anything like me, you just breathed a big sigh of relief. Knowing that Jesus is the author and finisher of our faith takes the pressure off. It is not up to us.

So, I ask you today….are you trusting in Christ as the author and finisher of your faith or are you trusting in your own efforts to produce faith in your life?

"Don't trust to hold God's hand; let Him hold yours. Let Him do the holding, and you the trusting."
~ Hammer William Webb-Peploe

Application:

- Rest in the fact that Jesus is the author and finisher of your faith. If you are struggling with your faith, come to Him. Only through a personal relationship with Jesus will you truly live a life of faith.

DAY 10

My initial goal was to go through the 21 days of faith challenge for 21 days in a row. However, I had an unexpected detour in this journey. A little over a month ago, I realized that I had an overuse injury from spending too much time working on the computer. My forearms were sore, my neck and shoulders were sore and I knew I needed to take a break from the computer. So for the past month, I have put this challenge on hold.

I have to admit that when I first realized my body was breaking down from overuse on the computer, my initial reaction was to worry. After all, my job now requires that I spend 90% of my day on the computer. So if I cannot use a computer, then I cannot work. If I cannot work, we may not be able to pay our bills. You can see where this quickly leads.

However, God immediately brought to my mind this faith challenge and I knew I wanted to handle this "crisis" differently and trust God to provide for us. So I brought the situation to God in prayer. As I did, I faced the fact that my body was not a machine and that

I was going to need to make some changes in order for my body to heal and for me to continue my work.

And an interesting thing happened.

As I faced the facts and surrendered them to God, emotions began to surface. I was no longer able to deny what was happening. I allowed myself to cry and grieve as I trusted God with my physical health and my finances. It was a healthy release of emotions. Instead of responding with worry and denial, I was able to feel my emotions and surrender the situation to God in faith.

And it made me think of one of the heroes of the faith that we read about in Hebrews 11. His name is Abraham.

Romans 4:19-22 says, "Without weakening in his faith, he (Abraham) faced the fact that his body was as good as dead—since he was about a hundred years old—and that Sarah's womb was also dead. Yet he did not waver through unbelief regarding the promise of God, but was strengthened in his faith and gave glory to God, being fully persuaded that God had power to do what he had promised. This is why 'it was credited to him as righteousness.'" (NIV)

So even as Abraham faced the fact that his body was as good as dead, he did not waver through unbelief regarding the promise of God that he would have a child but instead was strengthened in his faith. Amazing, isn't it? And that is how I want to respond as well. I want to be able to face the facts and yet not be weakened in my faith.

I want to respond by trusting God.

"Christians (as well as everyone else) have a tendency to try building a life in which faith is unnecessary. We establish a comfort zone where everything is in our control, but this is not pleasing to God. God will allow things into our lives that drive us to utter dependence upon him. Then we see His power and His glory."
~Henry Blackaby

Application:

- When a crisis comes into your life, what is your initial reaction? Is it worry, panic or denial? Or are you able to face the facts and trust God in faith with your circumstances?
- Write out the Scripture from Romans 4:19-22 and post it somewhere that you will see it every day. Read it every day and ask God to help you respond in a similar way the next time you face a crisis.

DAY 11

I was thinking the other day about things in my life that I put my faith in without questioning. For example, when I go to sit in a chair, I have faith in gravity. I also have faith that the chair will hold me as I put my full weight into it. When I eat my food each day, I have faith that it is not poisoned. I have faith each month that I will receive a royalty paycheck for my books that have sold.

So, if I can have faith in simple things like this, why is it difficult for me to have faith in God's promises? God shares His promises with us in His Word, the Bible. But do we really believe them?

2 Corinthians 1:20 tells us, "For all the promises of God in Him are Yes, and in Him Amen, to the glory of God through us." (NKJV)

What are some of the promises of God in the Bible? Here are just a few...

- Salvation comes through Jesus. (John 3:16, John 14:6)

- When we abide in Christ, we will bear much fruit. (John 15:5)
- We are heirs of God and co-heirs with Christ. (Romans 8:16-17)
- In this world we will have trouble, but Christ has overcome the world. (John 16:33)
- Jesus is the author and finisher of our faith. (Hebrews 12:1-2)
- Nothing can separate us from the love of Christ. (Romans 8:38-39)
- One day, in heaven, there will be no more death, sorrow, crying or pain. (Revelation 21:4)
- God who began a good work in us is faithful to complete it. (Philippians 1:6)
- God will provide for our needs when we put Him first in our lives. (Matthew 6:33)

I have learned that I can trust and have faith in the promises of God in the Bible. However, the first step for me was being able to trust the Bible.

"The Bible is a checkbook. When you said yes to Jesus Christ, many promises were deposited to your credit at that very moment, and they were signed by the Lord Jesus Himself. But now you have to cash your checks in order to profit by them.

When you come upon such a promise and say, 'Thank you, Lord, I accept this,' then you have cashed a check, and that very day you'll be richer than you were the day before."

~ Corrie ten Boom

Application:

• What you believe about God's Word, the Bible, will make a huge difference in how you live your life. So, today, reflect on this question…do you have faith in the promises of God through the Bible? Do you believe the Bible is absolute truth and has power for your life today? Or is the Bible simply a history book to you?

• Take a few minutes today to read the article I wrote several years ago about why I trust the Bible. I also share a song by Sanctus Real that has encouraged me titled "Promises." Read the article and listen to the song at: www.bodyandsoulpublishing.com/promises

DAY 12

As I have already shared with you, this last year was a difficult year for me. I finally realized that I needed to reach out for help. Our church offers free Biblical counseling and so I decided to set up an appointment. I ended up attending only two sessions, but God used them powerfully in my life.

During one of my sessions, I had an "ah ha" moment as we looked at the story of the feeding of the 5,000 in John 6:4-14 which you can read below.

"The Jewish Passover Festival was near. When Jesus looked up and saw a great crowd coming toward him, He said to Philip, 'Where shall we buy bread for these people to eat?' He asked this only to test him, for He already had in mind what He was going to do.

Philip answered Him, 'It would take more than half a year's wages to buy enough bread for each one to have a bite!'

Another of His disciples, Andrew, Simon Peter's brother, spoke up, 'Here is a boy with five small barley loaves and two small fish, but how far will they go among so many?'

Jesus said, 'Have the people sit down.' There was plenty of grass in that place, and they sat down (about five thousand men were there). Jesus then took the loaves, gave thanks, and distributed to those who were seated as much as they wanted. He did the same with the fish. When they had all had enough to eat, He said to His disciples, 'Gather the pieces that are left over. Let nothing be wasted.' So they gathered them and filled twelve baskets with the pieces of the five barley loaves left over by those who had eaten. After the people saw the sign Jesus performed, they began to say, 'Surely this is the Prophet who is to come into the world.'" (NIV)

We see that Phillip and Andrew had two very different responses to Jesus' question on how to feed the thousands of people that had gathered to hear His teachings.

1. Phillip looked at the facts and made statements based only on what he could see. "It would take more than half a year's wages to buy enough bread for each one to have a bite!"
2. Andrew surrendered the little resources he had to Jesus who then multiplied them to provide above and beyond what was needed.

Who do you relate to more in this story? For me, I relate more to Philip. I am naturally a problem solver and see the facts. I tend to look at a situation realistically and then try to figure out what it will take to get from A to B. However, this limits what God can do in the situation.

Instead, I want to be more like Andrew and in faith surrender the little resources I do have to Jesus and allow Him to multiply them. This does not mean that Jesus is a "genie in a bottle" to do my bidding. It simply means that I surrender my circumstances and what I do have to Jesus and then allow Him to take the lead. This also means that I am not limited by what I see but realize that Jesus is able to do more than I can ask or imagine. (Ephesians 3:20)

"God is not some little genie or a vending machine. And (He) is not just worth it because He makes your life all better, but He's with you. God wants so much more for your life than fine."
~ Jim Britts

Application:

•   In the story that we read above, do you relate more to Philip or Andrew and why?

- When faced with an impossible situation, I encourage you to approach it like Andrew did... bringing what you do have to Jesus and asking Him to do the rest. Then listen to God and obey Him. In the story above, the disciples were active participants in distributing the food. And in a similar way, God may ask you to take action in a specific way in your circumstances.

The Bible tells us that faith without works is dead (James 2:17). However, we want our actions to be led by God and not simply our own ideas. This means that we need to spend time in prayer bringing our requests to God, but also spend time in prayer listening to Him as well. This is very difficult in our fast-paced, media driven culture. However, spending time in silence listening to God is so necessary for a growing relationship with Him and a life of faith.

DAY 13

I want to share a picture that I believe God gave to me as I was meditating on the definition of faith recently.

Placing my faith in God is like handing my car keys to Him. I no longer have control, but look to Him for guidance. And because God now holds the keys to my car, He decides when we leave, He decides when to start the car, He decides where we go, etc.

And I have to admit, that as I think about this illustration, I feel uncomfortable. Why? Well, first of all, it is difficult for me to give up complete control. Secondly, it feels like I am doing nothing. I like to be an active participant and be able to do something.

But, it all comes back to trust. Do I trust God?

I need to know and believe that God does not want to destroy my life. On the contrary, He has a plan for me, to prosper me and not to harm me (Jeremiah 29:11). He wants to take me on the ride of my life...if only I will give Him the car keys.

The Bible says in John 14:12, "Very truly I tell you, whoever believes in Me will do the works I have been doing, and they will do even greater things than these, because I am going to the Father." (NIV)

When we decide to give the "car keys" of our life over to God and believe in Him in faith, He will do amazing things through our lives. Let's choose to live a life of faith and not miss anything He has for us!

"The world has yet to see what God can do with a man (or woman) fully consecrated to Him. By God's help, I aim to be that man."
~Dwight L. Moody (my insertion)

Application:

• Have you surrendered the "keys" of your life to God? Or are you still holding on and the one in control? Ultimately, Jesus does not want to simply be part of our lives, like one slice of pumpkin pie, He wants to be the main ingredient of our lives. He wants to be the pumpkin in our pumpkin pie. He wants to be Lord of our lives.

• Ask God if there is any area of your life that you need to fully surrender to Him. If you already have a personal relationship with Jesus Christ, then this could be a relationship, finances, your job, material possessions, your time, etc. Pray a prayer of surrender and visualize yourself handing the keys of your life in that area over to God.

However, if you have never surrendered your life fully to Jesus to make Him Lord of your life, I encourage you to do so today. There are many people that know about Jesus, can quote Bible verses and/or attend church regularly, but do not know Jesus on a personal level as their Lord and Savior. If that is the case for you, today can be the day of your salvation. There are no magic words to pray; you simply ask Jesus to forgive you of your sins, acknowledge that He is the only way to God, and then start living your life for Him.

If you do not know where to start you can pray this simple prayer: "Dear Lord Jesus, I know that I am a sinner and need Your forgiveness. I believe that You died for my sins. I want to turn from my sins. I now invite You to come into my heart and life. I want to trust and follow You as Lord and Savior. In Jesus' name. Amen."

If you are making this step for the first time, contact me and let me know. You can e-mail us by visiting our website at: Bodyandsoulpublishing. com/contact. We want to pray for you and send you some resources to help you grow in your relationship with Jesus.

If you want to know more or still have questions about a relationship with Jesus, I encourage you to read this article I wrote on my website at: www.bodyandsoulpublishing.com/jesus.

DAY 14

It can be easy to say that we trust in God, but how do we truly know that we are relying on Him?

My husband and I were short-term missionaries in the country of Belize, Central America for two years. When we arrived in Belize, we had a general idea of the ministry we would be involved in; however, we did not know the details of how everything would work out.

I remember the first few months as we were getting adjusted, we continued to pray for doors to open for us. We waited, and waited, and waited. At least that is what it felt like to me. During this waiting time, my husband, CJ, wrote out the following quote in big block letters and posted it on our kitchen wall where we would see it every day.

Here is the quote:

"Prayer is the proof we are relying on God."

And it is so true.

Prayer is the proof we are relying on God and not on ourselves. Eventually, my husband decided to undergo three days of prayer and fasting. During those few days of seeking God through prayer and fasting, God gave CJ a message that he then shared with over 10,000 Belizean students that year. Not only did God open the doors for ministry in schools in every district in Belize, He also gave CJ the opportunity to share a message about sexual purity that contained the gospel and impacted many lives. Prayer is powerful.

"Prayer is not asking. Prayer is putting oneself in the hands of God, at His disposition, and listening to His voice in the depth of our hearts."
~ Mother Teresa

"Any concern too small to be turned into a prayer is too small to be made into a burden."
~ Corrie ten Boom

Application:

- How is your prayer life? It is so easy to allow busyness to take over our lives, isn't it? I encourage you to spend intentional time connecting with God through prayer today. This could include a longer more intimate prayer time in the morning, short prayers all throughout the day, journaling out your prayers, etc. Then, continue coming to God day after day in prayer until it is a habit. Not a legalistic habit, but a habit that leads to a greater dependence and reliance on God...a habit that leads to a life of faith.

DAY 15

Today I want to share with you the story of Mary and Martha.

> "Now it happened as they went that He entered a certain village; and a certain woman named Martha welcomed Him into her house. And she had a sister called Mary, who also sat at Jesus' feet and heard His word. But Martha was distracted with much serving, and she approached Him and said, 'Lord, do You not care that my sister has left me to serve alone? Therefore tell her to help me.'
>
> And Jesus answered and said to her, 'Martha, Martha, you are worried and troubled about many things. But one thing is needed, and Mary has chosen that good part, which will not be taken away from her.'"
> Luke 10:38-42 (NKJV)

To be honest, I have always been able to relate to Martha. I am a hard worker and often have a long to-do list waiting for me each day. And some days, I neglect spending time with Jesus in order to start working on my to-do list. However, Jesus continues to remind me that the time I spend with Him sitting at His feet is so much more important than anything else.

It is similar to the story of a man chopping down a tree. He was working very hard, but not making much progress. Someone came up to him and realized that he was using a dull axe. They then recommended that he stop for a few minutes to sharpen his axe. However, the man pushed them aside saying he was too busy working to stop and sharpen his axe.

How foolish!

If he would simply stop and sharpen his axe, he would have finished his work much sooner. And the same is true in our lives when it comes to prayer. When we spend time in prayer "sharpening our axe," our day will often go so much smoother and more efficiently as we allow God to guide our actions and our thoughts.

"If I had six hours to chop down a tree, I'd spend the first four hours sharpening the axe."
~ Abraham Lincoln.

"I have so much to do that I shall spend the first three hours in prayer."
~ Martin Luther

Application:

• Have you spent time "sharpening your axe" through prayer today? Would Jesus say to you: "Martha, Martha, (insert your name) you are worried and upset about many things, but only one thing is needed. Mary has chosen what is better, and it will not be taken from her."?

Take time to sit at Jesus' feet today even if you only have a few minutes.

• I like to play instrumental worship music sometimes to help draw me into the presence of God.

DAY 16

In order to believe someone and have faith in what they say, we need to trust them. And when it comes to how we view God, our enemy, Satan, will try to plant doubt in our minds about God's goodness towards us. We see this in the Bible even as early as Adam and Eve in the Garden when Satan said, "Did God really say...?" Genesis 3:1 (NIV)

And sometimes our view of God can become distorted. What do I mean by this? I think of it like a carnival mirror that distorts our image of ourselves. We can choose to either look in a mirror to see who we really are or in the carnival mirror to see a distorted image of ourselves. In a similar way, we can choose to look into God's Word to see who God really is or we can allow our circumstances to distort our view of God.

Let me try to explain this way. By what we believe, it is as if we are putting on a pair of glasses by which we view the world. We can put on a Biblical worldview and see our circumstances through God, or we can put on our own glasses and see God through our circumstances.

Do you see the difference?

In one scenario we are putting God first and His Word is absolute truth in our lives. In the other scenario, we are allowing our view of God to be dependent on our circumstances and the things that happen in our lives.

I remember hearing someone tell a story of growing up in a pastor's home. He said many times people in the church would complain to him about his father. And he would tell them, "You don't know my father. I know him. I live with him and I see the sacrifices he makes for the church. I see when he gets up in the middle of the night to go and pray with a family in the hospital or when he takes a phone call in the middle of dinner to be there for someone who is hurting. If you really knew my father, you wouldn't say these things about him."

And I wonder how well we know our heavenly Father. Because when we know Him so well through His Word, then we will know that He is good. No matter what happens in our lives, we will be able to say, "I know my Father and I know that He is good. Even though I don't understand, I can trust Him."

How well do you know your heavenly Father today? In order to believe in Him and have faith in Him, you need to be able to trust Him and know that He is good, that He is a good God.

"Suffering provides the gym equipment on which my faith can be exercised."
~ Joni Eareckson Tada

"God's plan and His ways of working out His plan are frequently beyond our ability to fathom and understand. We must learn to trust when we don't understand."
~ Jerry Bridge

"If you look at the world, you'll be distressed. If you look within, you'll be depressed. If you look at God you'll be at rest."
~Corrie ten Boom

Application:

• Have there been circumstances in your life which have distorted your view of God? Or can you say confidently today, "I know my Father! And He is good." One way to get to know your heavenly Father is through His Word. For more resources to help you develop a healthy view of God, go to http://discovergod.com/character

- I experienced a difficult season in my life where my view of God became distorted. God gave me three pictures that helped me rebuild my faith and trust in Him that I share in my book, "Trusting God When Bad Things Happen."

DAY 17

God is teaching me that living a life of faith often means looking beyond what I can see with my human eyes. It can be easy to look at my life circumstances and jump to conclusions. However, things may not always be as they appear.

I encourage you to go back and read the story of Joseph in Genesis. It is a powerful story of God using the difficult times in Joseph's life for good. His brothers sold him into slavery. He ended up in Egypt and through a course of circumstances, he was put in charge of a project that would literally save those in Egypt and the surrounding countries, including Joseph's family, from starvation.

Joseph told his brothers who sold him into slavery, "You intended to harm me, but God intended it for good to accomplish what is now being done, the saving of many lives." Genesis 50:20 (NIV)

I can now see how God is using the painful experiences in my past for good. The enemy meant to harm and destroy me, but God is using it for good. And He wants to do the same in your life.

This poem describes it so well...

"The Weaver"
~Anonymous

My life is but a weaving, between my God and me,
I do not choose the colors, He worketh steadily,
Oftimes He weaveth sorrow, and I in foolish pride,
Forget He sees the upper, and I the underside.
Not till the loom is silent, and shuttles cease to fly,
Will God unroll the canvas and explain the reason why.
The dark threads are as needful in the skillful Weaver's hand,
As the threads of gold and silver in the pattern He has planned.

Application:

- Have you seen God bring good out of difficult times in your life? Write your answer to this question in a journal or discuss it with a friend.

- I encourage you to declare your trust in God through prayer. Feel free to use the prayer I have written out below or to pray a prayer from your heart.

Lord, I realize that I may never have all the answers to my questions this side of heaven. But, I ask that You continue to reveal Yourself to me, giving me wisdom and understanding. Help me to trust You with the things I still don't understand.

I thank You that You have promised to walk through every painful trial with me. That You will never leave me or forsake me. I thank You that even when other people fail me, You will never fail me. Help me to put my faith and trust in You and not in people or circumstances. I thank You that even if I can't see it, You promise to bring good out of the pain in my life (Romans 8:28). I love You, I worship You, I trust You. Amen.

DAY 18

Many times faith cannot be figured out, reasoned or analyzed. God does want us to use our intellect and the minds He has given us. But sometimes, when He asks us to do something in faith, it may not make sense in our human minds.

Simon Peter experienced this with Jesus in Luke 5:4-6. "When He (Jesus) had stopped speaking, He said to Simon, 'Launch out into the deep and let down your nets for a catch.' But Simon answered and said to Him, 'Master, we have toiled all night and caught nothing; nevertheless at Your word I will let down the net.' And when they had done this, they caught a great number of fish, and their net was breaking." (NKJV)

Simon Peter was a fisherman by trade and knew the ins and outs of fishing. He had been fishing all night and did not catch even one fish. It did not make sense to go back out and put his nets in the water again. However, did you see his response to Jesus?

Nevertheless at Your word, I will obey.

Nevertheless.

In saying this, Simon Peter was saying that he was choosing to submit to Christ instead of submitting to his own intellect and reasoning. We see a similar response from Jesus in the garden of Gethsemane prior to his death on the cross. He says, "O My Father, if it is possible, let this cup pass from Me; nevertheless, not as I will, but as You will." (NKJV)

Nevertheless.

How will you respond to God today?

"The man that believes will obey; failure to obey is convincing proof that there is no true faith present. To attempt the impossible God must give faith or there will be none, and He gives faith to the obedient heart only."
~ A. W. Tozer

"God is God. Because He is God, He is worthy of my trust and obedience. I will find rest nowhere but in His holy will, a will that is unspeakably beyond my largest notions of what He is up to."
~ Elisabeth Elliot

"God's commands are designed to guide you to life's very best. You will not obey Him, if you do not believe

Him and trust Him. You cannot believe Him if you do not love Him. You cannot love Him unless you know Him."

~ Henry Blackaby

Application:

- Even when it does not make sense or "add up" in your mind, are you willing to obey God and say "nevertheless"? Write out your response in your journal or discuss it with a friend.

DAY 19

Congratulations on making it to day 19 in this faith challenge. I pray that your faith has been strengthened and is growing each day through the empowerment of Christ. However, I wanted to take time today to remind all of us that even "if I have a faith that can move mountains, but do not have love, I am nothing."

I Corinthians 13:2b (NIV)

Faith – Love = Nothing

"And now these three remain: faith, hope and love. But the greatest of these is love."

I Corinthians 13:13 (NIV)

"'Teacher, which is the greatest commandment in the Law?' Jesus replied: 'Love the Lord your God with all your heart and with all your soul and with all your mind. This is the first and greatest commandment. And the second is like it: Love your neighbor as yourself. All the Law and the Prophets hang on these two commandments.'"

Matthew 22: 36-40 (NIV)

"Spread the love of God through your life but only use words when necessary."

~Mother Teresa

"I'm a little pencil in the hand of a writing God, who is sending a love letter to the world."

~Mother Teresa

Application:

- And the greatest of these is love. Ask God to fill you with His love today. Without love, your faith will mean nothing.

DAY 20

Several enemies to faith are doubt, worry, and fear. Many times they are planted in our minds through the lies of the enemy. The Bible tells us that our enemy, Satan, is the father of all lies and that there is no truth in him.

"You belong to your father, the devil, and you want to carry out your father's desires. He was a murderer from the beginning, not holding to the truth, for there is no truth in him. When he lies, he speaks his native language, for he is a liar and the father of lies."
John 8:44 (NIV)

What might these lies look like?

In the past I have taken the time to not only write out the lies that I believed, but also to write out the truth of what God says about it from Scripture.

I then write the truth on a notecard and carry it around with me. Sometimes I have needed to re-read the truth card multiple times throughout the day to fight the battle waging within my mind.

Here are two examples:

Lie: I cannot trust God because He has let me down in the past.

Truth: God is faithful and has my best interests in mind, even when I can't understand His ways. He will help me begin to trust Him again. He wants me to trust Him and I want to trust Him. (Lamentations 3:5-6; Isaiah 55:9; Proverbs 3:5-6; Psalm 91:1-3)

Lie: I am afraid of what the future holds.

Truth: God has plans for me - to prosper me and not to harm me, to give me a hope and a future. I can trust Him with my future. He is walking before me, preparing the way. (Jeremiah 29:11; Isaiah 43:18-19)

Practical Steps to Overcoming Lies with God's Truth

I want to share some practical steps God has used in my life to help me replace the lies of the enemy with God's truth.

Step #1: Recognize the lies. John 10:10

Step #2: Take your stand in the spiritual battle. Command Satan and his demons to leave in the authority of Jesus' name. When you resist the devil, he will flee from you. Ephesians 6:10-18, James 4:7

Step #3: Uproot the lie by confessing your sin of believing the lie (and any other sin you acted on because of the lie). I John 1:9

Step #4: Repent, asking for God's forgiveness for living your life based upon the lie. Luke 5:32

Step #5: Replace the lie with God's truth. Invite Jesus to come and the Holy Spirit to fill you with His truth (the opposite of the lie). John 8:32

"We're going to have to let truth scream louder to our souls than the lies that have infected us."

~ Beth Moore

Application:

• I encourage you to come up with your own truth cards. Search the scriptures using tools like www.BibleGateway.com, www.YouVersion.com or www.BlueLetterBible.org to find scriptures that relate to what you are going through. Re-word them into truths that you can carry with you and repeat until they replace the lies you have been believing.

DAY 21

It is hard to believe that today is the final day of this faith challenge. In closing, let's look at two obstacles to faith: unbelief and pride. We see both of these obstacles described in Luke chapter 9.

In the beginning of the chapter it tells us that Jesus gave His twelve disciples "power and authority to drive out all demons and to cure diseases, and He sent them out to proclaim the kingdom of God and to heal the sick."

Luke 9:1-2 (NIV)

Later in the chapter the disciples attempted to cast out a demon from one man's son. However, it says "they could not." (Luke 9:40). If they were given power and authority to drive out ALL demons, where did the power go?

Matthew 17:19-20 tells us what happened to their power. It was replaced with unbelief. "Then the disciples came to Jesus in private and asked, 'Why couldn't we drive it out?' He replied, 'Because you have so little faith. Truly I tell you, if you have faith as small as a mustard seed, you can say to this mountain, move from here to there, and it will move. Nothing will be impossible for you.'"

In Luke 9:41 Jesus addresses the disciples this way, "You unbelieving and perverse generation." (NIV)

How do you think the disciples were feeling after this evident failure on their part? What do you think they would be talking about?

Amazingly enough, "an argument started among the disciples as to which of them would be the greatest." Luke 9:46 (NIV) Instead of being humbled, they were talking about who was the greatest. Most likely, pride entered their hearts and replaced the power of God in their lives.

As you continue this life of faith, beware of these two obstacles: unbelief and pride. Any time you recognize these obstacles, confess your sin, repent, and then ask for God's empowerment through His Holy Spirit to truly live out a life of faith.

I pray that Jesus says to you, "According to your faith let it be done to you."

Matthew 9:29 (NIV)

"For with God nothing will be impossible."

Luke 1:37 (NKJV)

Application:

- How has God been working in your life throughout this 21 days of faith challenge?

  Write out your own story of faith in your journal, share what God has been doing in your life with a friend or share your faith stories in our private Facebook group here: www.facebook.com/groups/21daysoffaith.

APPENDIX

Definition of Faith:

One resource I use when studying the Bible is www.BlueLetterBible.org. Using their free online concordance, I looked up the word faith in Hebrews 11:1. Below, I have shared the definition of faith from Strong's concordance.

Pistis (Strong's G4102)

1. conviction of the truth of anything, belief; in the NT of a conviction or belief respecting man's relationship to God and divine things, generally with the included idea of trust and holy fervour born of faith and joined with it

   a) relating to God

      1) the conviction that God exists and is the creator and ruler of all things, the provider and bestower of eternal salvation through Christ

   b) relating to Christ

1) a strong and welcome conviction or belief that Jesus is the Messiah, through whom we obtain eternal salvation in the kingdom of God

c) the religious beliefs of Christians

d) belief with the predominate idea of trust (or confidence) whether in God or in Christ, springing from faith in the same

2. fidelity, faithfulness

a) the character of one who can be relied on

GET FREE CHRISTIAN BOOKS

Love getting FREE Christian books online? If so, sign up to get notified of new Christian book promotions and never miss out. Then, grab a cup of coffee and enjoy reading the free Christian books you download.

You will also get our FREE report, *"How to Find Free Christian Books Online"* that shows You 9 places you can get new books…for free!

Sign up at:
www.bodyandsoulpublishing.com/freebooks

Happy reading!

CJ AND SHELLEY HITZ

CJ and Shelley Hitz enjoy sharing God's Truth through their speaking engagements and their writing. On downtime, they enjoy spending time outdoors running, hiking and exploring God's beautiful creation.

To find out more about their ministry or to invite them to your next event, check out their website:

www.ShelleyHitz.com

Note from the Author: Reviews are gold to authors! If you have enjoyed this book, would you consider reviewing it on Amazon.com? Thank you!

OTHER BOOKS BY SHELLEY HITZ

Broken Crayons Still Color
A Life of Gratitude
A Life of Faith
Forgiveness Formula
Self-Publishing Books 101
Procrastination to Publication
Calligraphy for Beginners
Brush Strokes Workbook

And many more!

See the entire list here: www.ShelleyHitz.com

OTHER RESOURCES FROM SHELLEY HITZ

For Writing: Shelley is an author coach and has many resources for writers and authors.

Writing Week: a free 7-day writing challenge. Get started here: www.writingweek.com

Free Training: get all her free training for authors here: www.trainingauthors.com/free

For Creativity: Shelley is an artist and teaches online art classes.

Get started with three free classes here: www.yourcreativeadventure.com/free